CHESS OPENINGS FOR BEGINNERS

A Comprehensive Guide to Chess Openings

By Magnus Templar

Table of Contents

render any resulting actions solely under their purview. There are no scenarios in which the publisher or the original author of this work can be in any fashion deemed liable for any hardship or damages that may befall them after undertaking information described herein.

Additionally, the information in the following pages is intended only for informational purposes and should thus be thought of as universal. As befitting its nature, it is presented without assurance regarding its prolonged validity or interim quality. Trademarks that are mentioned are done without written consent and can in no way be considered an endorsement from the trademark holder.

Introduction

Congratulations on downloading CHESS OPENINGS FOR BEGINNERS, and thank you for doing so.

This eBook will introduce aspiring chess enthusiasts to the key concepts behind some of the most popular opening strategies. Concepts such as control of the center, pawn structure, open vs. closed positions, development, king safety, and transposition. Also covered is a brief overview of the tactics to know and watch out for during the earliest moments of the game. The readers will then be shown how all of these principles relate to some of the most popular openings in the game, such as the Italian Game, King's Gambit, Ruy Lopez, Queen's Gambit, and the English for white, and the Sicilian Defense, Caro-Kann Defense, French Defense, Italian Game, and Petrov's Defense for black. This book will take a look at some of the more popular variations, and how they differ from the mainline strategy. In some of these variations, it is possible for black to achieve an equality or even a possible advantage. The last part of the book will focus on how to continue improving beyond the scope of this book. This will provide readers with a foundation level understanding of Chess openings to build upon.

To learn more about the tactics mentioned in this book as well as other Chess strategies, be sure to check out the other book in this series: CHESS STRATEGY FOR BEGINNERS. As for now, learn how to master chess openings. Read on!

Chapter 1: Key Concepts to Chess Openings

Why Focusing on the Opening Matters

So you just bought this eBook entirely dedicated to chess openings, and you might be asking yourself: "Seriously? An entire book just for the *opening*?" Believe it or not, this book cannot even begin to scratch the surface of all the research and study that has gone into the opening moves of chess. The reason is simple: if you start the game better than your opponent you will have an advantage. In an ongoing effort to catch each other off-guard, even the most elite chess players diligently study the opening in order to be better prepared than their opponent.

In order to understand what's going on with the opening moves, there are a few important ideas we will need to cover first. They include control of the center, development, pawn structure, open and closed positions, king safety, and transposition.

We will introduce these concepts to you here in the first chapter so we can move on and apply them to some of the most popular opening lines in chess.

Navigating the Chessboard

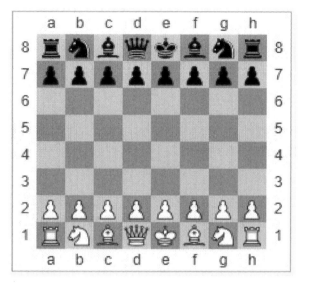

For the purposes of this book we will be using the standard algebraic notation for chess based on this chessboard diagram:

And according to this nomenclature:

Pawn = cell
Knight = N
Bishop = B
Queen = Q

King = K   Rook = R
Castle King-side = O-O
Castle Queen-side = O-O-O
Capture = x
Check = +
Checkmate = #
En passant = ep.
Promotion = c1=Q
Fantastic Move = !
Dubious Move = ?

Control of the Center

One of the goals of any opening of quality should be to gain control of the center squares of the board. We are mainly focusing on the **d4**, **d5**, **e4**, and **e5** squares, although **c4**, **c5**, **f4**, and **f5** are also important squares to consider as they help to control those four most important squares. The classic approach to the opening is to occupy these squares directly with pawns and to support them with your pieces. A more modern idea is to control the center indirectly with pieces, leaving pawns in a safer position and developing slowly. For the purposes of this book, we are going to be taking a look at classical approaches as they best illustrate the principles of controlling the center and developing quickly.

By controlling the middle of the board with our pawns we not only gain space to develop our pieces behind our pawns but will limit the mobility of our opponent, hopefully causing them to have to choose less ideal place for their pieces in order not to fall behind in development. We will cover development more in the next section but for now, just understand that another goal in the opening is to get as many of your pieces into action as possible while trying to stop your opponent from doing the same when possible.

Imagine for a moment you are white, and

you have a pawn on **d4** and on **e4** and your opponent hasn't moved yet. Can you see how your pawns create a wall blocking black's access to the center? White is attacking all of the black's side central squares: **c5**, **d5**, **e5**, and **f5**. Now if black were to try to occupy any of those squares, white can either defend the attacked piece to keep up the wall or exchange whichever they prefer. The point is that white has the choice about what happens and black has to play within that understanding. Now in a real game white doesn't get to move twice before black does, only once, but the principle is exactly the same. Because white has an ever so slight advantage by choosing the first move, they will always start the game with a small space advantage and time advantage (called a tempo) over black.

As such, white usually starts to play with confidence, staking a claim to the middle immediately and challenging black to find equality given white's inherent advantage.

Black, on the other hand, hopes to prove that white has overextended himself and gain equality in the position by taking his share of the space and winning back some of the lost tempi if possible.

It's time we take a look at the development and how to get our pieces moving in an effective way.

Development

When it comes to developing pieces of chess it must be said: Don't move the same piece twice without a good reason. Of course, this doesn't mean to pass up on great opportunities should they arise, nor neglect your defense if moving that piece is your best option. But generally speaking, you should aim to develop all your other pieces first before moving that same piece a second time if you can help it. If anyone has ever told you that you shouldn't bring your queen out early in chess, this is one of the key reasons why. The queen is incredibly powerful and as such is also very valuable. While it might be tempting to swing out your queen for a dramatic check early, chances are you are leaving your opponent with a valuable target to attack while also developing his own pieces. If you have to spend time running away while your opponent is making moves with his pieces, that actually means you are falling behind. For these reasons, most people develop their minor pieces first (knight, and bishop), and use their major pieces in supportive roles (Rook, and Queen).

In a typical opening from white, say:

1. **e4**

This move is the start of many famous chess lines and is fantastic for several reasons. First, this move directly stakes a claim on the center, by giving white control of the **d5** and **f5** squares. If you remember, those are two of the center squares that are very important for the opening. Also, by moving the pawn out of the way, it leaves white with several great options for turn 2. White has the option to develop either knight to great squares in **Nc3** or for the queen-side or **Nf3** and **Ne2** for the king-side. White could instead choose to deploy his light-colored bishop anywhere along the **a6-f1** diagonal. Finally, there is still the option to move another pawn, such as the popular King's Gambit.

For black, a typical response might be:

1. **e4**   **c5**

The Sicilian Defense, a popular answer by black to white's most common first move. This move stakes a claim in the center by occupying the **c5** square, and controlling the central **d5** square white might have been eyeing otherwise. If you remember the position where white had a pawn on both **e4** and **e5**, it created a real blockade for black to contend with. This simple flanking pawn maneuver gives black control of that central square by stopping that **d5** move from being played right away. Additionally, this move gives the black knight a great square on **c6** to occupy when it wants to. The **c** pawn has already moved ahead so the knight won't have to worry about getting out of the way for a future pawn advance.

Another general principle in the opening is to castle early. We will touch on this topic more in King Safety, but your opening moves should generally work towards preparing you to castle.

By following these steps, you will be making moves that have a purpose.

Pawn Structure

Let's imagine again that white has pawns arranged on **a2**, **b3**, **c4**, **d5**, **e5**, **f4**, **g3**, and **h2**. These diagonal formations of pawns are called **pawn chains**. Notice how each pawn behind defends and supports the pawn ahead of it. Pawn chains can be as small as two pawns chained together in a diagonal. These are power formations to use in order to give yourself a strong defensible position to play behind.

The next concept to consider with pawn structure is called **pawn islands**. Consider the same position as above but let's remove the **c4** and **f4** pawns, meaning, white has pawns on **a2**, **b3**, **d5**, **e5**, **g3**, and **h2**. Notice how white's pawns are separated into three separate groups? This means white now has three pawn islands. In general, the more pawn islands you have the weaker your pawns will be as they will be stretched thin, and unable to defend one another.

An **isolated pawn** is a single pawn as an island with no pawns on either side. Generally, isolated pawns are considered a weak point in the defense as only pieces can ever defend them. There are always exceptions of course, but generally, isolated pawns are something you hope to avoid.

Double Pawns or even **triple pawns** can occur, which is just a fancy name given when two or even three pawns end up on the same file. In most cases, these pawns are considered a weakness as the pawns on the same file cannot help protect each other.

A **backward pawn** is a pawn that cannot be safely advanced and is behind all pawns of the same color. In a hypothetical position with white with a pawn on **e4** and black with pawns on **d6** and **e5**, the black pawn **d6** would be backwards if there is no pawn on the **c** rank, as it cannot safely advance, or it will be captured by white's pawn on **e4**.

Finally, a **passed pawn** is a pawn that no enemy pawn is able to stop, as it has "passed" their attack range. In a position with white having a pawn on **e4**, it would be a passed pawn if no pawn on either the **d** or **f** file could stop it from advancing to promotion.

Open and Closed Positions

Open positions arise in openings where central pawns are exchanged and the center becomes more accessible. As the name suggests these positions are filled with open spaces and long diagonals. As such, rooks, bishops, and the queen all shine in these kinds of games, as they can best take advantage of the spaces.

Closed games are games where the pawns are still on the board, usually locked in a potential exchange, going many layers deep.

These games are highly tactical and involve thinking many steps ahead in exchanges to determine who the potential victor would be in a big exchange in the middle. The theme of closed games is very often maintaining the tension, as many times the person who gives in to the pressure and attacks first, comes out behind. In closed position, knights tend to shine a bit more as they are capable of maneuvering themselves around the tight battlefield better than most other pieces.

King Safety

It was mentioned before in the development section, but for the most part, your opening moves should work towards enabling you to castle. If you develop pieces on both sides of the board before castling your king, you are opening yourself up to potentially devastating all-in attacks at very early turns in the game. The most extreme example of this is called the **fool's mate**, and it is the fastest way to lose a game of chess. If you were curious:

1. **f3 e5**
2. **g4?? Qh4#**

However, it doesn't need to be so extreme as that in order to run into problems. Many exciting professional chess matches were decided by gutsy sacrifice attacks made against a king stuck in the middle of the board. Such is chess, but for beginners, it is always best to start by keeping the defense of your king in mind.

This ties into the last point on king safety, and that is the pawns around your king. It is rarely a good idea to advance the three pawns in the corner you want to castle unless you really have to. Any time you advance one of these pawns you are creating a tiny weakness in the defenses around your king that your opponent can later try to use to attack you.

Transposition

Many openings have similar elements to them and can be reached in different move orders. Being able to move from one opening into another is called transposition, and is one of the ways great players can stay flexible in their opening moves while sticking to the same overall opening plan. In response to your opponent's moves, it might be preferable to change your move order, but that doesn't mean you have to go off into uncharted territory. Look for ways to transpose from your deviation back into a position you are familiar with. This is how the best players can play chess in positions they are unfamiliar with. They make reasonable moves looking to go back into familiar territory.

Chapter 2: White's First Moves

King's Pawn Opening / The Open Game

Known as the King's Pawn Opening, this is by far white's most popular choice historically and empirically. **1. e4** has proven a favorite opening move by some of the biggest names in chess. It is easy to see why as the move accomplishes all of the main goals we set out for our opening. It controls the key central squares **d5** and **f5** as well as allowing development of two of our pieces, the bishop, and the knight. It is for this reason that it should come as no surprise that three of our example openings are King's Pawn mainline variations. When black replies back with the move **1...e5** this is called the Open Game.

King's Gambit (1. e4 e5 2. f4)

A historically very popular opening, especially around the 19th century when this opening saw a lot of play. It has since fallen out of favor somewhat but is still worth mentioning to beginners as it keeps to our core opening principles and has a lot of solid theory and evidence to support its success.

The main line starts off:

1. e4 e5
2. f4

Immediately white contests the center with the sharp pawn advance **f4**. A little bit of lingo here for this opening: *a gambit is a sacrifice for some other advantage.* In this position, black can simply capture the pawn on **f4** immediately if they so choose as white is not defending their **f4** pawn. There are two main variations to the King's Gambit depending on whether or not black accept this sacrifice. They are therefore named the **King's Gambit Accepted** if black chooses to take the pawn on **f4**, or the **King's Gambit Declined**, should black instead choose to protect their now threatened **e5** pawn. Let's start off with the King's Gambit Accepted to try and learn why white would ever want to give a pawn away in the first place.

King's Gambit Accepted

With the moves:

1. e4 e5
2. f4 exf4

We have reached the first position in the King's Gambit Accepted. It is white's turn to play now. If you remember back to our discussion about controlling the center, white was very happy to have pawns on both **d4** and **e4** as this gave them very excellent control of the middle of the board, as well as options for all of their minor pieces to develop naturally. We will cover what **d4** brings to the table in a lot more detail in the Queen's Gambit Opening. This is the most usual continuation for white, but sometimes white will instead elect to play **Nf3** followed by **Bc4** next turn to both stop black from advancing their **f4** pawn, as well as to prepare to castle immediately.

King's Gambit Declined

After:

1. e4 e5
2. f4 bc5

This is the King's Gambit Declined – Classical Defense. Black has developed his bishop, as well as interfered with white's attempt to castle – as you cannot castle through check. You may be wondering why white wouldn't simply capture the black **e5** pawn after black neglects to protect it. Let's take a look at what happens if white takes the pawn.

1. fxe5?? Qh4+

Suddenly white is in some real trouble. They are either going to lose the rook after:

2. g3 Qxe4+

Notice how both the King and the Rook are being attacked? This is a tactic called **a fork**. Because black has forked white's king and rook, black is going to have to move his king and lose the rook.

If instead, white tries to run, the game ends swiftly:

Ke2   Qxe4#

We will take a deeper look into the King's Gambit during the next chapter.

Italian Game (1. e4 e5 2. Nf3 Nc6 3. Bc4)

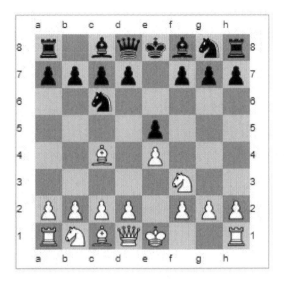

A historic opening, containing over 500 years of recorded games, it has been studied by many of the biggest names in chess history. The characteristic move of this opening is the move:

1. e4   e5
2. Nf3 Nc6
3. Bc4

Sometimes referred to as the Italian Bishop. These games are very often sharp attacking games with white trying to focus on the poorly defended **f7** square (only the king defends it at the start of the game).

Also note how white has started developing an attack while, at the same time, preparing to defend with a castle king-side at any moment. A hallmark of high-level chess is accomplishing several goals with just one move.

Black, on the other hand, will usually try a strong counterattack in order to try and prove white was overzealous in their efforts. While more modern variations such as the Ruy Lopez have gained popularity, it is still worth examining this opening as there are great attacking chances for both sides. The two main variations branch depending on how black decides to respond after white moves their bishop. After **3...Bc5** we reach a position known as the **Giuoco Piano** and after **3...Nf6** we instead reach a position called the **Two Knights Defense**. We will be exploring each one separately.

Giuoco Piano

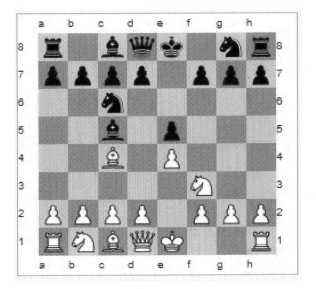

The Giuoco Piano main line continues as follows:

1. e4 e5
2. Nf3   Nc6

3. Bc4   Bc5 - Giuoco Piano with Bc5
4. c3

White is playing **c3** in order to prepare the move **d4,** grabbing vital central spaces away from black. Black will usually try to either counterattack with the aggressive move **4...Nf6**, or hold on to their central control with the move **4...Qe7**. Note that while this is a queen move in the early game, it doesn't violate our opening principles here, because the queen is being used far back on the 7th rank, as a support for her more forward pieces. This is a great and safe way to activate your queen without putting her in immediate danger.

Two Knights Defense

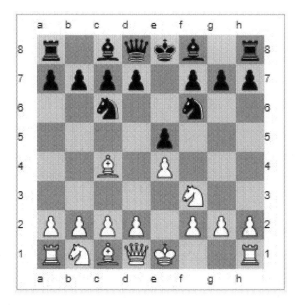

The Two Knights Defense starts out with:

1. e4 e5
2. Nf3   Nc6
3. Bc4   Nf6

The most obvious attacking continuations is to continue with the move **4. Ng5**. White is increasing the pressure on that **f7** square and threatening to win a pawn by force, as well as messing up black's hopes of castling. The usual reply from black is:

4.4 Ng5   d5

From this position, white has little option but to take on d5 as his bishop and e4 pawn are both under attack. After this, there are several different variations we will discuss later on.

However, black can instead try the exciting move:

4. Ng5   Bc5

This is a dangerous counterattack from black. He is ignoring the mounting pressure upon the **f7** square in favor of developing some counterattacking potential. White has three main variations: **5. d4**, **5. Bxf7+**, and **5. Nxf7**.

Ruy Lopez (1. e4 e5 2. Nf3 Nc6 3. Bb5)

It can be said that the Ruy Lopez is the go-to option for many professional chess players when it comes to the Open Game (1 e4 e5). Unless black plays with perfection, it can be very tough for them to achieve equality. This is one of the key reasons why many black players choose to use the Sicilian Defense in response to **1. e4** instead. We will be covering that opening in the section for black in Chapters 4 and 5 if you're interested in learning how that plays out.

After **3. Bb5,** let's take a moment to analyze the relationship between white's bishop and black's knight. Imagine for a moment that the pawn on **d7** didn't exist or had already moved to **d6 or d5**. If you notice, white's bishop would attack black's knight and have the king lined up right behind it. This maneuver is called **a pin**. Pinned pieces can't move or they will expose a valuable piece of it (King, Queen or Rook usually, but pawns can be pinned to other pieces too!) to danger. Black someday has hopes of making a break in the center with a move like **d5**, but with the white bishop attacking the black knight, that is an issue for black to think about. Let's see how black typically likes to respond:

1. **e4   e5**
2. **Nf3 Nc6**

3. **Bb5 a6**   - Morphy Defense

Named after the great chess player Paul Morphy during the 1800's, this is the most popular response for white.   This move forces white to clarify their intent with the move **b5**. If he wishes to trade bishop for knight, black has taken no steps to prevent this exchange. If white retreats back to **c4** black has won a tempo back from white by forcing him to move his bishop twice.

The most common line is called the **Closed Defense** and goes as follows:

4. **Ba4 Nf6**
5. **O-O Be7**

Ba4 from white to retreat away from the attacking pawn. Note that black can still, at any time, kick the bishop away with the move b5. In some variations, the white bishop may find itself trapped in the corner and care must be taken to allow room to escape a possible **b5** pawn thrust by black at any moment. **Nf6** increases black's central pressure by attacking the **e4** pawn, as well as supporting that **d5** move black has in the back of their mind. White castles away to safety and black develops his bishop and prepares for a king-side castle of his own.

Queen's Pawn Opening / Closed Game

White starts the game off with the great move **d4** and achieves several of our goals for the opening. White again occupies a central square with a pawn and attacks the two important central squares in **c5** and **e5**. Also, white can now look to develop their queen-side bishop as the pawn has moved to allow the bishop to move. It's a bit far away yet, but this move does also contribute to king safety in the sense that it is the first of several moves that white could use to facilitate a queen-side castle.

Although there are several good replies for black, very often black will choose to occupy his central space with a pawn on **d5** and there the Close Game has been reached. All the same good things that applied for white, apply to black as well, so black feels very comfortable in staking a claim in the center in this way. Next, we will explore a mainline called the Queen's Gambit. One of the oldest and most exciting chess openings, as it features exciting chances for both sides.

Queen's Gambit (1. d4 d5 2. c4)

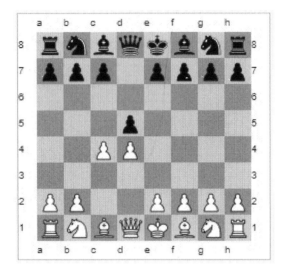

The Queen's Gambit is one of the oldest studied openings with well over 500 years of written history to support it. Another gambit opening which, if you remember from the King's Gambit, means some kind of sacrifice in material for a positional advantage.

Play starts out:

1. d4   d5

2. c4

Right away, white is telling black that he intends to fight for the middle in a serious way. He is offering an undefended wing pawn on **c4** in exchange for that ever-tempting double pawn center of **d4** and **e4**. The difference is, unlike the King's Gambit that takes place on the relatively undefended king's side, this gambit takes place on the queen's side and that means the queen can get involved much more readily if the need arises. Because of this difference, it is not a true gambit, as black can't actually hold on to their pawn on **c4** after the exchange, which we will cover below. Just like the King's Gambit, the Queen's Gambit has two mainline variations depending on whether or not the offer on **c4** is accepted by black, and they are called **Queen's Gambit Accepted**, and **Queen's Gambit Declined**. We will cover each variation in some detail.

Queen's Gambit Accepted

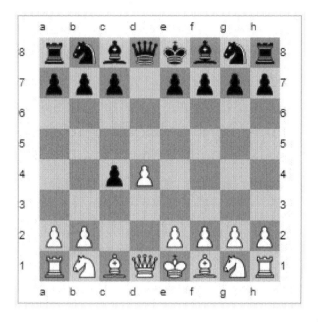

To recap, the position is:

1. d4   d5
2. c4   dxc4

The Queen's Gambit Accepted has been reached after these set of moves. As I promised you earlier, this was not a *true* gambit and I told you that black can't hold on to their current pawn advantage. Let me first demonstrate that to you now.

3. e3   b5?

The move **e3** is played if white aims to recapture the pawn immediately, as it opens up the light-square bishop onto the **c4** square, threatening the opponent's pawn already. Also, it helps solidify white's center which can be useful in ensuring that white's plan goes off without any interference from black. The play would continue:

4. a4   c6?
5. axb5 cxb5?
6. Qf3!

After that dazzling queen move, black is going to lose a piece. This isn't the main line but I wanted to show you how black's best chances are to accept that the pawn isn't going to stay around and play objectively good chess instead.

White's most common play here is actually **3. Nf3**.

White recognizes that the pawn on **c4** is doomed and instead focuses on getting a slight lead on development. White will usually move to recapture the c4 pawn in their upcoming turns as follows:

3. Nf3   Nf6 - Black's most common reply is to develop their own knight
4. e3   Nc6
5. Bxc4   c5
6. O-O

This position leaves both players with solid chances. White has regained their missing pawn and has developed their pieces to effective spaces. Black, on the other hand, managed to get through the opening with equality in terms of development and space and should feel satisfied with his chances of going into the later stages of the game.

Queen's Gambit Declined

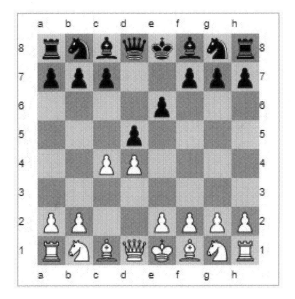

While technically, any move that is not **2...dxc4** is considered a Queen's Gambit Declined game, we will be focusing on the orthodox response as follows:

1. d4   d5
2. c4   e6

By moving his pawn to **e6,** black is able to defend his central pawn, holding on to his control of the center. In addition, this allows black the option to develop his dark-squared bishop along the **a3-f8** diagonal, also getting him one step closer to eventually castling to safety king-side.

While this is a solid and defensible position for black to play from, and indeed many players with the black pieces have found success here, white will try to prove that black's light-squared bishop does not have an effective square to find a meaningful place in the game. Black, on the other hand, will try to either release the bishop, trade it off, or find a useful supportive outpost for it and try to use it in the end game.

Another option for black to try is **2...c6** which is called the **Slav Defense**, which we will examine from black's point of view in an upcoming chapter.

The main line continues thus:

    3. Nc3 Nf6
    4. Bg5 Be7
    5. Nf3

White develops his queen-side knight to its ideal square behind the c4 pawn where it can exert great control over the middle of the board. Black takes the opportunity to get his king-side knight into the game and help prepare his king-side castle. White tries to take advantage of black's last move by creating a **pin** on black's knight onto the queen. Black is forced to develop his dark-squared bishop to **e7** to free black's knight from this pin (now if the black knight moves, the bishops will face off instead of leaving the queen exposed).

White then develops their knight to a good square and helps solidify the bishop's position on **g5** against a potential

discovered attack from the knight against the previously undefended bishop. A **discovered attack** is when the movement of one of your pieces will expose an attack from another piece behind it. These maneuvers are an excellent tactic to watch out for as it can come as a real shock to an unsuspecting opponent (or you if you get caught in one yourself!).

c4 – English Opening

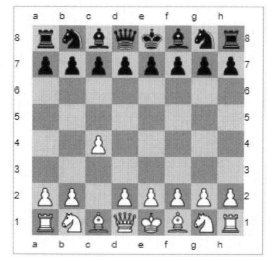

While the move has been known since antiquity, it only arrived in tournament level play in 1843. Considered a somewhat new opening, this was an opening used by such legends as Bobby Fischer in his sensational match against fellow legend Boris Spassky.

It is known as a **flank** opening, meaning it attempts to exert control over the center of the board from a wing pawn position. Wing pawns are the pawns on the **c** and **f** files for both sides. The **c4** pawn in the initial position controls the **d5** square of our opponent with a non-central pawn. If we could trade our **c** pawn for our opponent's **d** pawn, we would have a slight advantage, since we could then play **d4** and control space with our pawn, that our opponent has to use pieces to have the same control. These are small advantages, but they can add up when you keep gaining more small advantages. This is how professional chess players win.

One feature about the English Opening, in particular, is that it is a flexible opening that can transpose between other well-known positions or stay on its own unique path. This flexibility is one of the big draws for players who enjoy this opening, as it allows them to play a very adaptive style of game in response to what their opponents are trying to do.

This opening has two main lines called the **Reversed Sicilian**, or the appropriately named **Symmetrical Defense**. This opening is much less rigid than some of the other openings we looked at before, and generally has some goals it tries to achieve and less a strict order of moves. Nonetheless, we will take a look at very common move orders here to go over the strategy behind the opening.

Reversed Sicilian

The line starts out:

1. c4   e5

The name of this variation comes from a very popular black opening called The Sicilian Defense, which we will cover in black's section of this book. Take a moment to look at the formation of black in that section if you wish. The way that games usually continue after this opening is:

2. Nc3 Nf6
3. g3

The knight development to **c3** is again perfect since the **c4** is already moved. Black likely wants to prepare to king-side castle and solidify their stake to the middle so **Nf6** is perfectly reasonable. But then there is this odd **g3** move. This move seems to break one of the rules we laid out about king safety and pawn structure. We normally don't want to move any of the three pawns around the side of the board we plan to castle. While this move does weaken the pawn chain itself by opening diagonals through **g2**, what white is intending to do is a maneuver called **fianchettoing-the-bishop**. This fancy word really just means you will be putting your bishop into that hole you just opened up in **g2**. This diagonal on the board is called the **long diagonal** and is a great outpost for bishops, as it gives them the most possible squares that they can move to.

From here black can play either **3...c6** or **3...g6** with both having about equal chances. With that being said, white will almost always follow up with **4. Bg2**.

Symmetrical Defense

As the name suggests, the line begins:

1. c4   c5

Black holds on to positional symmetry with this move. White has many options of play and many of them are tried. The moves white wants to play in some order are **g3** and **Bb2** when possible. Additionally, the queen-side knight would be quite happy on **c3** since the pawn has already advanced. And finally, the king-side pieces need to be developed to allow castling. These moves can really be executed in the most logical sequence based on your opponent's moves, but for the sake of demonstration we will show a typical move sequence here:

2. Nc3 Nc6
3. g3   g6
4. Bg2 Bg7
5. Nf3 Nf6
6. O-O O-O
7. d4

Now that's a lot of moves all in a row, and they are all keeping perfect symmetry, but it doesn't have to happen exactly like this. The important thing to recognize is what the position looks like, and you can do the moves leading up the castle in a different sequence. In games where black just keeps mirroring white, black is neither falling behind nor gaining ground. It tends to be a line that can lead to positions more likely in ending in a draw, with white being given slightly better odds due to moving first.

Chapter 3: Black's First Moves

e4   c5 - Sicilian Defense

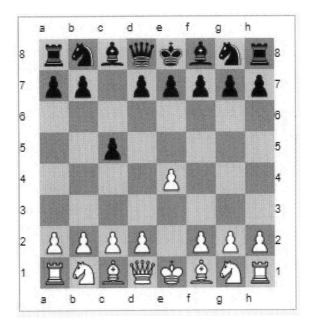

Easily the most popular and statistically successful opening for black to the nearly universally played **1. e4** from white. While visually similar to the English Opening: Reverse Sicilian, this is a much older opening with a full and rich history. Indeed, enough has been said on the Sicilian to fill several books in their entirety with this opening alone. Let's start by analyzing the opening move from black **c4**.

Just like in the Reverse Sicilian for white, black aims to control the center of the board from a flanking wing pawn, keeping their important **d** and **e** pawns for a potential break in the middle later. Again, if black could ever trade their **c** pawn for white's **d** pawn, he could see that as a slight advantage over white, as he could then have a central pawn majority over the white player. As we have seen before, the advanced **c** pawn also provides a great outpost for black's queen-side knight that is a major factor in how the game usually plays out.

From a theoretical standpoint, black is starting to lay a claim to the dark-colored squares in the center of the board. Imagine for a moment that black could achieve their goal of a Knight on **c6** as well as the eventual move **e5**. Notice the grip that black would have on all those central dark squares. The **c** pawn gives control over **b4** and **d4**, the hypothetical pawn on **e5** targets the **d4** and **f4** dark squares, and a knight on **c6** could exert its influence on **a5**, **b4**, **d4**, and helps protect **e5**. This is a very common theme for black to try and have a rock-solid grip on the dark squares, especially **d4**, where white would otherwise have plans of eventually making a break with moves like **c3** and **d4**. Lastly, to further show dark-square dominance, a common strategy for black will be to **fianchetto** their dark square bishop at **g7** giving them even greater control over those squares.

There are two mainline variations to the Sicilian Defense, called the Open and Closed Variations. Let's take a look at the Open Sicilian first:

Open Sicilian Defense

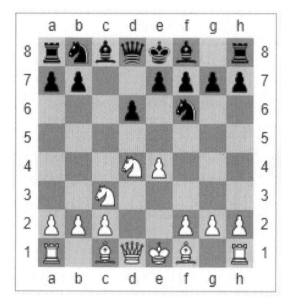

The main Open line goes as follows:

1. **e4   c5**
2. **Nf3 d6**
3. **d4**

White develops their king-side knight, preparing to castle shortly. White is also taking a chance to control more of the center of the board, especially those dark squares we know black is so keen on in **d4** and **e5**. Black has other options for his second move other than **d6**, however, this is the most common reply. The move **d6** by black creates a pawn chain with the **c5** pawn, solidifying the defense of that pawn. Additionally, it opens a path for the light-square bishop to activate along the **c8-h3** diagonal. Finally, this move actually prepares black to play their king-side knight to **f6**. Notice how if black played the knight move immediately, as in **2. Nf3 Nf6**, white could cause some real problems for black with the simple move: **e5**, threatening to capture our freshly developed knight and taking a lot of central space. Best to avoid that scenario with the preparatory move **d6.**

There are of course many other ways black could respond after **Nf3** which we can touch on in the next chapter. From here the main continuation is:

3. d4   cxd4
4. Nxd4   Nf6
5. Nc3

Black has achieved one of his goals of exchanging his **c** pawn in for white's **d** pawn. Black continues to develop the king-side knight now that white can't disturb it with their **e** pawn because of the **d6** pawn protecting the **e5** square for us.   White continues development with **Nc3**.

In this position, black will try to prove that his central pawn majority is winning and has a clear advantage.   White, on the other hand, has a significant lead in piece development, as well as more control over the center of the board, which he will argue, giving him more than fair compensation for his **d** pawn.

Closed Sicilian

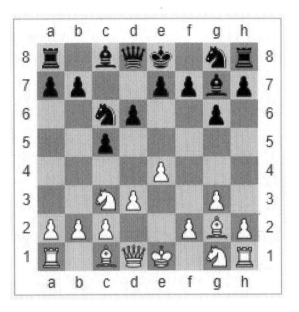

The main line looks like this:

1. e4   c5
2. Nc3 Nc6

And here black will develop similarly to in the open Sicilian but not always in the same order.   Black has goals they wish to accomplish and not a rigid plan of attack requiring a strict move order.

We want that knight on **c6** and usually, we want our bishop to fianchetto on **g7** (Notice how the black pawn chain is otherwise in the way for black to put their bishop on a meaningful square. Fianchetto is a great way to solve this problem!). We get our queen-side knight into the game on its favorite square now as well. This is a great example of why knights like to be behind pawns. Look at the difference between the two knights on the **c** file. Notice how black's **c** pawn has contributed to his plan in a significant way. White would love to be able to play moves like **c3** and **d4** and grab some of that juicy center, but right now his knight on **c3** is in the way! This is one of the major draws for players who enjoy playing flank openings such as the English and the Sicilian.

Let's see what is considered to be the main line, but again this move order can vary significantly:

3. g3   g6
4. Bg2   Bg7
5. **d3   d6**

Both white and black have the same idea here: My pawns are in the way and I need to get my king-side bishop into the game somehow. Once again, a fianchetto is the answer, and in this case, both sides will usually opt for this strategy, as they are both being walled in by their pawn chain. White's pawn on **e4** is still on the way – for now. White can at any time open a **discovered attack** with a cheeky move like **e5**, both attacking black's pawn chain (assuming it is played after **d6** from black), and disrupting the scope of black's bishop.   Both sides solidify their pawn structure by creating pawn chains in turn 5 with **d3** and **d6** respectively.

From here both sides will develop their last pieces and castle, and we have reached a stable and about equal position to start a mid-game. Both sides have great chances here and many fantastic positional games have been reached from this opening.

e4 e6 - French Defense

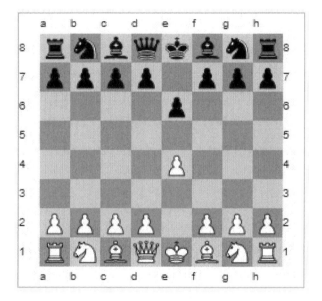

The French Defense is a fairly recent opening that began to see more prominent play in the early 1800s. This is a bit of a slower start compared to some of the more flashy openings and can lead to some very technical closed games.

The main line opens as follows:

1. **e4   e6**
2. **d4   d5**

White gets his classical double pawn center, but black intends to fight back from the very start with an early pawn advance on **d5** supported by his first move **e6**.

White has several responses. The most popular is **3. Nc3** to protect the attacked **e4** pawn.

Another common try is **3. Nd2** called the Tarrasch variation which is similar to the usual move **3. Nc3** in that it defends **e4**, but also different in the sense that the knight has a broader scope for its second move, and the dark-squared bishop has been blocked in, meaning it cannot be developed until a solution is created.

There is another variation known as the Advance Variation, where white plays **3. e5** taking the space given by black's second move and avoiding the exchange of central pawns.

Finally, there is the exchange variation that can be tried after **3. exd5 exd5**, which leads to a symmetrical pawn structure, with each player having a pawn on **d4** and **d5** respectively. The exchange variation leads to a position that is objectively equal for both sides, and either side will have to try to unbalance the position if they hope to achieve a win instead of a draw.

Winawer Variation

Let's take a look at **3. Nc3** and a typical continuation of the main line called the Winawer Variation now, as it is one of the most well-studied continuations for the French Defense.

3. Nc3   Bb4
4. e5   c5
5. a3   Bxc3+
6. bxc3 Ne7

Let's walk through each move. White moves his Knight to **c3** protecting the **e4** pawn. Black moves his bishop to **b4** creating a **pin** on the **c3** knight against the white king. This pin effectively means that **e4** is no longer defended as that knight cannot move to recapture while pinned to the king, as it would leave the king in check, an illegal move.

To deal with the undefended pawn, white advances it to **e5,** claiming some extra space, and making a pawn chain with **d4**. Black seeks to undermine this pawn chain with the pawn move **c5** attacking the **d4** pawn, protecting the **e5** pawn now. White aims to dislodge the bishop on **b4** with the move **a3**, by attacking the bishop with a lesser piece, making black decide what they want to do.

Black captures the knight on **c3** and white recaptures with his **b** pawn, creating **doubled pawns** for white to worry about later. Finally, black develops his king-side knight to a square preparing to castle soon. White is still several moves away from being able to castle and if black castles and breaks things open in the middle, white can find himself in a real danger being caught in the middle of the board with his king.

This variation is a very good try for black to achieve equality or possibly an advantage. He is exchanging a slightly cramped space by virtue of white's **e5** pawn, for a lead in development and better king safety.

e4 c6 - Caro-Kann Defense

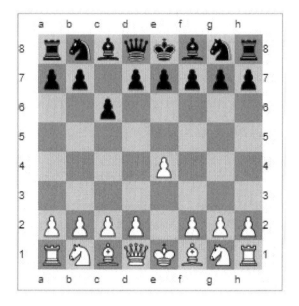

Compared to some of the big-name chess openings like the King's Gambit and the Italian Game, the Caro-Kann Defense is a very newly adopted opening by chess masters, only entering into professional play in the late 1800s.

From the initial position, white will almost universally play **d4**, to claim the classical **d4** and **e4** center white loves so much. Black's plan with **c6** was to prepare for turn two and the move **d5**. Black immediately contests white for the middle. This tension makes many newer white players uneasy and results in an early exchange, which favors black. Since if white is the one to initiate the exchange black will end up trading the **c** pawn for white's precious **e** pawn.

By preserving both central pawns in the event of an exchange, black hopes to avoid some potential weaknesses found in some other openings when playing for control of the center directly with a move like **e5**.

By creating this tension on **d5** it forces white to clarify his intentions and allows black to react accordingly. There are three main ways white tends to reply and these are the main variations of the Caro-Kann. They are the **exchange variation**, either of **Nc3** or **Nd2** as they very often transpose into each other, and the **advance variation** where white pushes their pawn to **e5**. We will take a quick look at the exchange variation and the **Nc3/Nd2** line in this chapter. The advance variation plays very similar to the French Defense with some positional differences to consider.

Exchange Variation

This line starts out as follows:

1. e4   c6
2. d4   d5
3. exd5 cxd5

Black strikes back into the center with **d5** and white chooses to trade pawns. The next moves vary but the most common line and considered the main line goes like this:

4. **Bd3 Nc6**

White develops their bishop to **d3**. The main purpose of this move is to control the **f5** square, preventing black from developing to its light-squared bishop to its optimal square on **f5**. The next moves can vary. But, to finish off the main line for the exchange variation, a common continuation is:

5. **c3   Nf6**
6. **Bf4 Bg4**
7. **Qb3**

White makes a solid pawn chain with c3 and limits the potential scope of black's dark-squared bishop by taking away the **b4** square. Black develops their king-side knight to better defend the king-side squares, including **g4** which will be important in a moment. White develops their dark-squared bishop to a useful square on **f4**. And black take advantage of the support of their knight on **f6** to play **Bg4** attacking white's queen while developing to a useful square. Finally, white will move the queen to safety and develop to a useful square by moving her to **b3**. This move gives her excellent scope over the board, including the now weak **b7** pawn, since the black's light-color bishop is now sitting on **g4**.

From this position, we have reached an equal position with both sides having roughly equal chances.

Nc3/Nd2 Variations

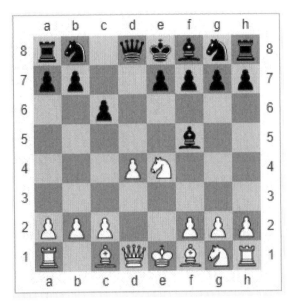

This line is considered together since they will usually transpose into the same position after black plays the move, **3...dxe4,** and white recapturing with the knight at either position moving to be on **e4.** This is where the line begins:

1. **e4**   **c6**
2. **d4**   **d5**
3. **Nc3/Nd2 dxe4**

4. Nxe4

The classical variation then continues:

4. Nxe4   Bf5
5. Ng3   Bg6

Black attacks white's undefended knight after the capture, and so white retreats to **g3** and now attacks the bishop! The black bishop retreats to **g6** to stay in a good position and get out of harm's way.

There is actually a special relationship here between black's bishop, and white's knight that is pretty annoying for white to deal with. A bishop that is 4 squares away from a knight (eg. Bg6 and Ng3) can cover every square the knight can move forward.

Because of this reason, white will sometimes continue with the idea of eventually disrupting that bishop with **6. h4**. Black will usually respond with **6...h6** giving the bishop a spot to back into if needed, and stopping that **h4** pawn from disrupting black's pawn structure.

The main line goes like so:

6. **h4**	**h6**
7. **Nf3**	**Nd7**
8. **h5**	**Bh7**
9. **Bd3**	**Bxd3**
10. **Qxd3**	

Both sides activate their knights, black wants to get into the action king-side so it deploys to **d7**. White continues on with his pawn on the **h** file, moving up a square. Black tucks his bishop away in the corner where it will be safe as well as to shore up the space left behind by the move **h6**. White plays **Bd3** – a final challenge to that pesky light-colored bishop for black: Capture me or I will capture you and leave your king more exposed. Black is forced to trade bishops, and white will collect the annoying black bishop once and for all with **Qxd3**. From here we have a position where black can hope to have some solid defensive options in the mid-game without having conceded too much to our opponent in terms of positional weakness.

e4 e5 2. Nf3 Nf6 - Petrov's Defense (Russian Game)

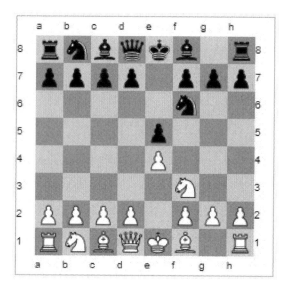

Also known as the Russian Game, this is a

symmetrical response that became more popular after it was introduced by Alexander Petrov in the mid-1800s. It is a favorite by many who prefer to avoid the Sicilian Defense, and it also steers white away from common lines such as the already demonstrated Italian Game and the Ruy Lopez.

Classical Variation (3. Nxe5)

Let's take a look at the classical variation:

1. **e4   e5**
2. **Nf3 Nf6** - Petrov's Defense
3. **Nxe5   d6**

Note that it is a mistake for black to try and mimic white with a recapture of their own, as white will come out ahead in position or material. Instead, black should dislodge the knight on **e5** to force it to move with the simple move **d6**. Let's see what happens if black tried to capture with **3...Nxe4**.

3. Nxe5   Nxe4?
4. Qe2

And now white either wins black's queen (4...Nf6??   5. Nc6+) after a **discovered attack** with the knight moving to strike at the queen, or gains a much better position after **4...Qe7 5.Qxe4 d6 6.d4 f6 7.Nc3 dxe5 8.Nd5 Qd6 9.Bf4 Nd7 10.0-0-0**.

Instead, black plays the move **3...d6** taking the central space with his pawn, supporting with that knight on **f6**.   Mainline play continues:

4. Nf3 Nxe4
5. d4   d5
6. Bd3

White brings his knight back to safety, black now takes the opportunity to capture white's pawn with **Nxe4**.   Both white and black fight for the middle with central pawn advances to **d4** and **d5** respectively. And finally, white tries to increase the pressure against the advanced knight on **e5** with his bishop moving to **d3**. It will take white a couple more pieces if he hopes to come out ahead with an exchange of bishop and knight, as if white is not careful and simply exchanges pieces now, it could be black that ends up with a large space advantage. If they get a pawn on **e4** supported by moves like **f5** and **g6**. Black could then tuck his king away queen-side instead, and be left with a brilliant mid-game to look forward to with a nice spatial advantage.

Steinitz Variation (3. d4)

This variation progresses as follows:

1. **e4**   **e5**
2. **Nf3** **Nf6**
3. **d4**

From here black can capture either pawn. If pawn takes pawn, the line would go:

3. d4 exd4
4. e5 Ne4
5. Qxd4 d5
6. exd6 (ep.) Nxd6
7. Nc4 Nc6
8. Qf4

Black captures pawn for pawn with **exd4**, white advances his **e** pawn further to **e5**, threatening the knight on **f6**. The knight moves to a more central square with **Ne4**. White wants to continue having central control and so scoops up black's hanging pawn on **d4**. Black plays **d5** to protect the knight on **e4**, supporting itself from the black queen on **d8**. White exchanges with **exd6 (ep.)**.

En Passant, meaning "in passing" in French, is a special move that happens when a pawn tries to run past another pawn like we just seen. In the turn **right after** the pawn runs past, the other player will have a one-time opportunity to capture the pawn as it passes.

Knight captures back with **Nxd6**. Next, we continue with development on the queen-side with **Nc4** and **Nc6** respectively. Finally, white activates their queen to **f4** pressuring black's somewhat exposed king-side. This is a pretty even position for both sides.

If black decides to capture with knight instead, we would have the following:

3. d4	**Nxe4**	
4. Bd3	**d5**	
5. Nxe5		**Nd7 or Bd6**

Here, black captures the **e4** pawn instead with his knight. White again adds pressure against the **e4** knight – a real theme in the

Petrov, and black defends with **d5**. White captures black's pawn now with the move **Nxe5**. And now black can continue development with either **Nd7** or **Bd6** as both help to increase black's control of the center, while also developing pieces. Notably, the Bd6 option allows black to castle.

d4 c5 2. c4 c6 - Slav Defense

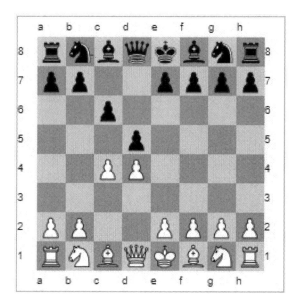

As mentioned in a previous chapter, the Slav Defense is one of the main ways black can play against the Queen's Gambit. If you remember from our discussion during the Queens Gambit Declined, one of the problems black could face quite often was having his light-colored bishop end up trapped behind the pawn chain. Another possible weakness of traditional defenses when it comes to the Queen's Gambit Declined is that the traditional black's pawn structure is left with clear targets for white to focus on during the mid-game. The Slav Defense is an attempt to deal with these issues as black.

The main line looks like this:

1. **d4   c5**
2. **c4   c6**
3. **Nf3   Nf6** - 3...e6 is an opening called the Semi-Slav
4. **Nc3   e6/dxc4/a6**
5. **a4   Bf5**

Everything looks normal – both sides are developing in a usual manner, white choosing often to deploy both knights back to back in turns 3 and 4. Black has three usual moves to choose from on turn 4.

As mentioned, the move **e6** transposes into an open known as the Semi-Slav. This central pawn move is to maintain a solid pawn chain after an eventual pawn exchange on **d5**. If you notice, however, one drawback with this position is that the black pawns trap the light-colored bishop, and black may struggle to find meaningful game-play with that bishop.

The next possible choice is the pawn exchange with **dxc4**. White is happy to trade their wing pawn for a central pawn, the main point of the Queen's Gambit. The usual follow up here would be **5. a4** to stop black from trying to reinforce the advanced pawn on **c4** with the move **b5**. The typical next move for black is to develop the bishop to **f5**, preventing white from pushing the pawn to **e4** next turn.

The last option for turn 4 **a6** plays into the same idea for black: an early **b5** play to add increased pressure onto the queen-side. Black aims to follow up very shortly with **b5**, and even if white tries to hold on to his space temporarily with a move like **c5**, after **b6** we see that black is going to start tearing down that center one way or another.

One of the reasons players have begun to favor **a6** is because it does not create that problem for the light-squared bishop becoming inactive. Black can keep the **c8-g3** diagonal open and find scope for the bishop soon.

Chapter 4: What's Next?

Okay, so we just learned a whole bunch of moves for both white and black that only get us to move 5 to 10 or so. What next? How do we proceed from here when we are swimming in unknown waters? Welcome to the mid-game. These are the uncharted waters that chess players try and navigate to actually *win* a game of chess. When you reach the end of your opening knowledge, this is called playing out of the book, and there are a few key ideas to keep in mind to help guide you along your way.

Know the End-Game

This is probably the other most important area to study in chess. Considered dry by many in the chess community, the study of the end-game mostly involves rote memorization of mating patterns. While not the most exciting area of study, being able to recognize a winning position from 6 moves away can certainly help you get through the otherwise uncertain parts of the mid-game. If you can master an extensive list of moves in the opening, and you can recognize mating patterns from several moves away, you are chipping away at the unknown part of the game for you to have to play in.

At a minimum, you should work to be able to checkmate a king on the open board with each of the possible pieces to do so. Some are as simplistic as they come, such as Queen and King. Others can prove a challenge for even a seasoned player of the game, such as checkmate with two bishops and a knight, is not an easy task to be sure.

The study of the end-game is far too broad a topic to include here in this chapter, however, so be sure to look for other resources on this topic to improve your game.

Know the Tactics

Unlike a broad and fuzzy topic like, *What strategy should I use to win?* tactics are tools to know in your chess toolbox. They are pieces you can learn to recognize both for yourself and from your opponent. Using tactics allows you to gain an edge in position, material or time (tempo). We have already introduced the **fork**, **pin**, and **discovered attack**, but let's include the full list and briefly explain the rest. The tactics to know include:

- Pins
- Skewers
- Overloading the Defender
- Zugzwang
- Forks
- Discovered Attacks

- Sacrifices
- Zwischenzug

For reference, we will define these tactics here once again.

- **Pins** are when your attack on the front piece is lined up with another more valuable piece behind it, making it disadvantageous to move the pinned piece. A good general rule to follow is to attack the pinned piece.

- **Skewers** are very similar to pins, except reversed. The attack is against a high-value target such as the king or queen, with another usually undefended piece lined up behind it. When the high-value target has to move out of the way, you have an attack against the piece behind.

- **Forks** are the knight's specialty, although, in truth, any piece can deliver a fork attack. Forks occur when with one move you attack more than one of your opponent's pieces. Usually, this can involve a check against the king while threatening some other piece that is typically lost.

- **Discovered Attacks,** we have already touched on, but they happen when the movement of a piece exposes an attack onto another piece. This is often done with a knight moving to attack deep into enemy positions, exposing a threat from a bishop, rook, or queen behind it.

- **Overloading the Defender** is a bit of a different tactic but the essential boils down to looking for pieces that are overworked and focusing there. In an arbitrary example, if a knight is a vital defender of, say, the **e4** pawn and is also a vital defender of a bishop on, say, **d5,** that knight is overloaded and can't protect both. You can use this to your advantage by attacking one side and having another attack prepared for the other piece after the knight is forced to respond.

- **Sacrifices** are attacks in which the attacker will lose an attacking piece or pieces without any material as compensation. The reason for these often flashy, reckless looking attacks is to expose an otherwise weak position to its breaking point. Sometimes by making a sacrifice attack, you can create such an instability in the opponent's position, that even down material as you are, they cannot possibly hope to defend against the force you can bring down on them. Some of the great immortal games of chess are exciting sacrificial attacks such as this.

- **Zugzwang**, a German term meaning "compulsion to move," is an idea that may sometimes force your opponent to move can lead to an advantage. Especially in king and pawn vs. king endgames, this principle often makes the difference between a win and a draw. Often in chess, the simple concept of giving away a tempo can lead to an advantage.

- **Zwischenzug** is another German term, this time meaning "intermediate move". The principle is that sometimes in a lengthy exchange that both sides have seemingly calculated deeply, there can exist a Zwischenzug or in-between move that catches the other person completely off-guard, and changes the entire dynamic of the position. This can be something obvious like a check that brings the exchange to a screeching halt, a big flashy sacrifice, or even a quiet move that just slightly alters the position in such a way that the calculation now favors the other player. Definitely one of the subtler concepts to know, but worth covering nonetheless.

Learn about the Principles of Chess

In the second book in this series, CHESS STRATEGIES: For Beginners, we will be focusing on strategy and tactics. One of the key strategic elements it will cover is some of the core principles of chess. If you've played the game for any length of time you will hear some old adages of advice such as "knights on the rim look dim", and "passed pawns must be pushed". There are many more of these gems of advice to learn. More importantly than just knowing these principles, however, is being able to understand them, and apply them to your game.

Chess Puzzles

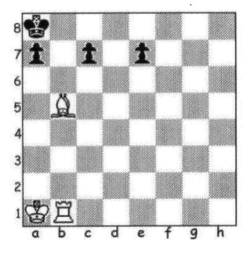

The study of chess can become a bit dry and tedious at times if you just stare at a chessboard and a reference to study. One of the ways chess players have found to improve is to create chess puzzles and challenging each other to find a solution to a clever position.

The puzzle on the right is a very simple example of a type of puzzle called "Mate-in-One", where the puzzle asks the player to find the next move to win the game. There are some puzzles that are much more complex and can stump even some of the best names in chess. The point of these puzzles is not to puff your chest and say how much you know, but to get you thinking about the game in new ways, and hopefully help your brain to recognize some winning positions due to being familiar with a similar position from a puzzle you've completed. They really work! And more importantly, they can keep things fun so you don't get bored while trying to learn.

Join a Chess Club

No, seriously, join a chess club in your area! This is a great way to meet new players and probably new friends too. Most major cities boast at least one major chess club and cater to players of all skill ranges. They host kids' events for young children, as well as tournaments for those wishing to test their competitive mettle. The local chess club is a fantastic resource to learn about the game and to meet potential coaches and mentors that are willing to help you grow as a player.

Find a Mentor

Along with joining a chess club, you can try and find a mentor; someone from a local chess club or tournament with some experience that is willing to take you under their wing, and show you some cool tricks and tips about the game. These people can offer you a literal lifetime of knowledge to draw upon and are *invaluable* to you as a growing player.

Play in a Local Tournament

Along with joining a chess club, this is another great way to enter into the exciting world of chess in a big way. At a local tournament, you will meet players of *all* skill levels, and it is another fantastic way to make chess friends and learn about the game. After playing a match for real in a tournament you will find others to talk to about your matches and learn about ways you could have played differently and different ideas for next time. Also, because you are playing several games back to back with time in between, it's a great way to try something, learn some new skills after your game, and apply those new skills in your very next round.

Some of the biggest names in chess history found their start in a small local tournament that grew into a passionate love for the game.

Conclusion

In summary, this book discussed the importance of controlling the center and developing quickly, the role our pawns play in safety and offense, as well as some key tactics to know and watch out for. Next, we put that knowledge to use in exploring some key openings to know such as the Italian Game, King's Gambit, Ruy Lopez, Queen's Gambit, and the English for white, and the Sicilian Defense, Caro-Kann Defense, French Defense, Italian Game, and Petrov's Defense for black. We talked about how to improve your game beyond the material provided in this book. Finally, we also touched on a few concepts for further study such as Chess puzzles and a study of the end-game.

Thank you for making it through to the end of CHESS OPENINGS: For Beginners, let's hope it was informative and able to provide you with a basic understanding of Chess openings, and their underlying principles.

As you have read, chess is a game for everybody. It's a great game that enhances thinking skills and strategies.

For those wanting to learn more, the next step is to download the other book in this series: CHESS STRATEGY FOR BEGINNERS. The focus of this book will be on the fundamental tactics and strategies to know to improve your game. Tactics such as pins, forks, skewers, discovered attacks, overloading the defender and more. Also covered are key strategic principles including light and dark squares, good and bad bishops, playing from behind vs. when ahead, pawns, sacrifices, and much more! Take your chess playing to the next level with these crucial skills.

Dear reader,

I sincerely hope that you enjoyed CHESS OPENINGS FOR BEGINNERS and could increase your understanding of Chess. Before you close this book I´d like to ask you for a favor to leave an honest review on amazon. It´d be greatly appreciated.

Thank you and good luck!
Magnus

Summary

To the beginning chess players, it can be an overwhelming experience trying to learn and improve your game. There are so many possibilities and combinations that all your pieces can move! CHESS OPENINGS: For Beginners is able to provide the reader with a starting place to begin their Chess learning. We will start with learning the basics: the center of the board is the most important, we want to develop quickly and effectively in our first few turns, and the importance of our pawns. Next, we will discuss king safety and how straying from those basic principles can leave us in trouble. To round things out we will cover transposition or moving from one opening into another one, as well as some important tactics to look out for. We will focus on explaining these principles of the game in such a way that it makes sense and relates to the openings we will be focusing on. The book will cover the openings move by move, giving relevant notes about the position, key concepts, and ideas, as well as noteworthy pitfalls to watch out for. Variations of the main line are discussed as well as some reasoning behind these different choices. Finally, we will talk about how to continue growing as a chess player, and where to look to keep learning. We encourage readers to join the chess community and become a lifelong player of the game of Chess.

CHESS OPENINGS: For beginners analyzes some of the most popular openings in Chess. For white, we will focus on the Italian Game, King's Gambit, Queen's Gambit, the Ruy Lopez and the English. These openings all focus on strong middle control and offer flexibility in terms of their gameplay and position. Notably, there are both open and closed possibilities as well as one flank strategy. For the black pieces, we will focus on the ever-popular Sicilian Defense and several of its many variations. Additionally, we will cover the French Defense, Slav Defense, Caro-Cann Defense and Petrov's Defense. Each of these positions gives black solid chances for counter-play while sticking to the core principles we want to focus on: controlling the center and developing quickly. We will examine a few variations on each line as well as noteworthy transpositions along the way. Finally, we will show how the lines can develop in the midgame with a couple noteworthy examples.

Features:
- Introduction to key concepts such as control of the center, pawn structure, open vs. closed positions, tactics, development, king safety, and transposition.
- Move by move explanations for some of the most popular openings in the game

- Italian Game, King's Gambit, Queen's Gambit, the Ruy Lopez, and the English for white.
- The Sicilian Defense, French Defense, Slav Defense, Caro-Cann Defense and Petrov's Defense for Black.
- Several variations are covered and discussed for each mainline
- How to evaluate a position objectively
- What to look for when determining your opponent's plan
- How to create a strong plan for your own

57059965R00061

Made in the USA
Columbia, SC
04 May 2019